HIJACK

by

Bernice Rubens

SAMUEL FRENCH, INC.

45 West 25th Street   NEW YORK 10010
7623 Sunset Boulevard HOLLYWOOD 90046
LONDON   TORONTO

IMPORTANT BILLING AND CREDIT REQUIREMENTS

All producers of HIJACK *must* give credit to the Author of the Play in all programs distributed in connection with performances of the Play and in all instances in which the title of the Play appears for purposes of advertising, publicizing or otherwise exploiting the Play and/or a production. The name of the Author *must* also appear on a separate line, on which no other name appears, immediately following the title, and *must* appear in size of type not less than fifty percent the size of the title type.

CHARACTERS

OSCAR ANDERSON, a publisher

DEBORAH WOOLAND, his secretary

HARRIET ANDERSON, his wife

VICTOR, a writer

KRISHNA, a cleaning person

TIME & PLACE

The action takes place in a London publisher's
office over a long bank-holiday weekend.

4

HIJACK

ACT I

Scene 1

Friday evening. A publisher's office.

Center backstage is a desk, and at right angles to it, a secondary one. Opposite, a couch, draped with an ornamental cover. The walls are book and file-lined, and the furnishings are plush. Exit left leads to the street down a flight of stairs. Exit right leads to the secretary's office. The front section of the stage houses the "insert stage." This is merely a raised platform and is lit only for the scenes inside "the book."

OSCAR ANDERSON sits at his deck. HE is a man in mid-forties, balding slightly, but otherwise wearing well. HE is leafing through a manuscript. From outside the street door, we hear a repeated intoned MANTRA. OSCAR listens for a while, contemptuously mimicking the sound. After a beat, enter KRISHNA, the "Hari Krishna" cleaner. HE is purple-robed with a mane of hair falling from an otherwise bald scalp. HE carries a cleaning-tidy in one hand and a hoover in the other.

OSCAR. You're early, Krishna.

KRISHNA. Well it's Easter weekend. Thought you'd have left by now.

OSCAR. Still some work to clear up. You going away?

KRISHNA. Going to the retreat for a couple of days.

OSCAR. You must tell me about that place.

KRISHNA. (*Settling on corner of desk.*) Well it's a ...

OSCAR. I don't mean now. Next week maybe.

KRISHNA. Well I'm only here till Wednesday. Then Alice comes back. Have to find another temp. Try a solicitor's firm next, I think. Like to learn about the law.

OSCAR. Have you learned a lot about publishing?

KRISHNA. Picked up a few tips here and there.

OSCAR. Listen, I'll be here for another hour. Just do the post room and the stairs.

KRISHNA. If you say so. (*HE goes out, starting on a mantra.*)

OSCAR. (*Listens for a while.*) Lunatic!

(*His BUZZER rings.*)

DEBORAH. (*V.O.*) It's Warren Peters for you. Are you in?

OSCAR. Good God no. Say I've gone away. (*Pause.*) Oh and tell him I've taken his novel with me. (*To himself.*) Like hell I have. (*HE rises and sifts through a pile of manuscripts on the floor by his desk. To himself.*) Warren Peters ... Peters ... (*HE picks up one of the manuscripts and opens it on the first page. Reading.*) "The surprising introduction of the quadrophonic element in the Gregorian chant has puzzled musicologists since the dawn

of time." (*Long pause.*) "Hubert said." (*To himself.*) He
calls it a novel.

(Enter DEBORAH, pretty and in her twenties.)

DEBORAH. He was pretty furious. He said you've had
his book for three months. Is it so terrible?

OSCAR. I haven't read it. But I've *weighed* it and it
weighs bad.

DEBORAH. Here's the paperback contract for the bird
book. (*SHE puts a sheaf of papers on his desk.*) Have you
told her yet?

OSCAR. (*Hesitant.*) No.

DEBORAH. You've left it a bit late.

OSCAR. (*Irritated.*) I know.

DEBORAH. Well are we going or not?

OSCAR. Of course we're going, sweetheart. I've got
the tickets. Here, take yours. Air France terminal. 8:30.
Don't be late.

(Pause.)

DEBORAH. When are you going to tell her? You've
guests to dinner tonight. (*Losing her cool.*) Are you going
to tell her before or after? Or maybe during dinner.

OSCAR. Sweetie, don't worry. I'll tell her. I've just
got to choose the right time.

(PHONE rings. DEBORAH picks it up.)

DEBORAH. (*Into phone.*) Hullo? Er … er … yes. He's
tied up I think. (*To Oscar.*) It's your wife.

OSCAR. What the ... what's she doing here?
DEBORAH. Now's the right time perhaps.
OSCAR. Jesus!
DEBORAH. I'm getting out of here.
OSCAR. (*Resigned.*) Tell her to come up. Er ... just give me a minute, will you.

(*Exit DEBORAH. OSCAR sits at his desk then rehearses to himself.*)

OSCAR. I've got a sudden meeting in Paris, Harriet, dear. An auction ... I ... er ...

(*A sudden idea prompts him to pick up the phone. HE speaks into it, rehearsing again. KNOCK on the door.*)

OSCAR. (*Loudly.*) But that's very short notice Monsieur Savarin. (*Aside.*) Come in.

(*Enter HARRIET, a handsome, well-dressed woman in her forties. OSCAR puts his hand to his head in mock despair, and motions her to sit down.*)

OSCAR. (*Into phone.*) But is it not possible for next week? I had arranged to go to the country with my wife. It really is very inconvenient. (*Pause.*) Of course I want to be at the auction. When does Monsieur Boudin go to the States? (*Pause.*) Then it'll have to be tomorrow. (*Shrugs at Harriet.*) There's a plane at nine I think. I'll be in your office at about eleven. We'll have to work through Sunday. And Monday if necessary, tell him. Au revoir. (*HE puts the phone down. To Harriet.*) Did you hear that? No Dorset for me this weekend. Oh I'm so sorry darling. (*Pause.*) I've got a present for you.

HARRIET. It's not my birthday.

OSCAR. I can give you presents can't I without it being your birthday?

HARRIET. I don't know why Oscar, but whenever you give me a present, I feel ... er ...nervous.

OSCAR. (*Nonchalantly.*) Why?

HARRIET. I look at my dresses sometimes. My bags, scarves, jewelry. Your sundry gifts. Each one of them marks the beginning of one of your philanderings. I've got a wardrobe chock-a-block full of your conscience.

OSCAR. You're pretty ungrateful, aren't you. Well here it is. (*HE practically throws it at her.*)

HARRIET. (*Furious.*) Don't you turn the tables on me, Oscar. This isn't your first present don't forget. There was that mohair stole in the name of one Penny. There was that little grey chiffon number when Amanda took Penny's place. To say nothing of the mink stole that followed. God, your conscience must have really pricked you on that one.

OSCAR. (*Weakly.*) You're talking nonsense.

HARRIET. (*Tartly.*) I had to wait ages for my next little gift. What was it? Oh yes, it was on a certain Deirdre's behalf. You gave me a very indifferent scarf. Poor Deirdre. She must have been a one-night stand. And what have we here? (*SHE opens the package.*) Ah, a pretty little gold bracelet. You must have high expectations of this one, Oscar.

OSCAR. You ungrateful bitch.

HARRIET. I suppose you'll deign to come home for dinner. We have guests you may remember.

(Pause.)

OSCAR. Why did you come, Harriet?

HARRIET. I've got the car downstairs. Had a weak kindly moment. Thought you might like a lift home.

(OSCAR goes toward her and puts his arm round her shoulder. Against her will, SHE responds.)

OSCAR. I've still got a contract to go through. It'll take me an hour.

HARRIET. Mrs. Smith will be furious. She spent half the morning sorting out your fishing clothes for the weekend.

OSCAR. Tell her I'm sorry.

HARRIET. You'll have to tell her yourself on Monday. I'll be gone by the time she comes tomorrow.

OSCAR. Tuesday maybe. It depends how long it takes.

HARRIET. Well you usually get what you want.

KRISHNA. *(Puts his head around the door.)* I'll be off now Mr. Anderson. Do your office on Tuesday.

OSCAR. Have a nice weekend.

KRISHNA. You too, Mr. Anderson. *(HE leaves.)*

OSCAR. Lovely boy, that one, but so mixed up. Wish I could help him.

HARRIET. *(Smiling.)* You're not all bad, Oscar.

OSCAR. *(On happier keel.)* Can you open the claret as soon as you get home.

HARRIET. *(Switching mood.)* Oh yes, Harriet will open the claret. Harriet will preside at table. Harriet will wear your gold bracelet, and everybody will think we're a very happy couple.

OSCAR. (*Pleading.*) Give me time, Harriet.

(HARRIET laughs bitterly and leaves. OSCAR sits at his desk, his head in his hands.
After a beat, enter DEBORAH.)

DEBORAH. I didn't listen but it sounded terrible. All that bit about the wardrobe.

OSCAR. (*Angry.*) You weren't listening of course. It's none of your business anyway.

DEBORAH. Now look ...

OSCAR. Don't you start too. (*Pause.*) Everything's arranged. We're going to Paris for the weekend ... (*Without conviction.*) we're going to enjoy ourselves.

DEBORAH. We don't have to, you know. You can go to Dorset for the weekend. I can go my own way. (*Pause.*) And I don't have to come back.

OSCAR. Don't you threaten me, Deborah. Even Harriet doesn't do that.

DEBORAH. That's why you're safe. That's why you never have to make a decision.

OSCAR. (*Roughly.*) Come here.

(SHE crosses to him and HE takes her in his arms.)

DEBORAH. How long are we going to go on like this?

OSCAR. Give me time, sweetheart.

DEBORAH. (*Laughing.*) It's becoming a joke. I've been giving you time for three years.

OSCAR. It's not easy you know. But look, let's have a wonderful weekend, with just each other.

(SHE settles for that.)

OSCAR. What time is it?

DEBORAH. You can decently pack up. It's almost 5:30. I've seen to the lights and I've switched the phone through.

OSCAR. I still have work on this contract.

DEBORAH. (Kissing him.) Tomorrow then. Got to wash my hair, press my going-away suit. Early to bed.

(OSCAR grabs her, but SHE disentangles herself and leaves.
OSCAR returns to the perusal of the contract, humming to himself. After a beat the PHONE rings. HE picks it up.)

OSCAR. Hullo? Hullo? (Purring sound.) Damn.

(HE puts the phone down and resumes his reading. FOOTSTEPS outside the door. OSCAR looks up, puzzled. The steps are followed by sounds of WEIGHTS being lugged up the stairs. OSCAR grows nervous. HE rises tentatively and inches his way towards the door. HE is nowhere near it when it bursts open.
Blazing on the threshold stands VICTOR, mid-thirties, and clearly a nutter. HE holds a gun in his hand which HE levels at Oscar's head.)

VICTOR. Don't move.

(OSCAR stands rooted, shit-scared. VICTOR motions to someone outside the door.)

VICTOR. In here.

(A cardboard carton is kicked into the room. Then another. VICTOR shoves them forward with his foot. Finally a hamper.)

VICTOR. Thanks. *(HE hands some money to the unseen cabbie, then kicks the door shut.)*
OSCAR. *(Trembling.)* What do you want?
VICTOR. Your time.
OSCAR. Well ... of course. Sit down. *(HE inches back to this desk.)*
VICTOR. Don't move. *(HE goes to the desk, opens all the drawers. Frisks Oscar's body, and is satisfied.)* Now *you* sit down.

(OSCAR does so, trembling. VICTOR crosses to the cartons. Levelling the gun with one hand, HE bends down and undoes the carton with the other. From it, one by one, HE extracts eight lots of manuscripts and puts them in a pile on the smaller desk. Then HE places them in order in a single line. OSCAR gets the message.)

OSCAR. Jesus!
VICTOR. And there's another lot like that one.
OSCAR. What are they?

VICTOR. What is *it*, you mean. It's my novel. Three thousand pages.

OSCAR. It's a ... a long book.

VICTOR. It's long and it's good.

OSCAR. (*Eagerly.*) I'm sure it is. *Very* good. I'll read it. Is that what you want?

VICTOR. I told you. I want your time.

OSCAR. Well of course.

VICTOR. I want it *now*.

OSCAR. But I ...

VICTOR. Yes I know. You're busy. You've got a dinner party at your house tonight. You're off to Paris tomorrow with your secretary. I've done my homework.

OSCAR. How did you ... ?

VICTOR. I told you. I've done my homework.

OSCAR. But I can't ...

VICTOR. (*Raises the gun ever so slightly.*) I've planned it all. You'll ring your wife. You'll tell her that you've been called to Paris immediately. There's a plane at ten o'clock. Tomorrow you'll phone the airport and you'll leave a message for your secretary.

OSCAR. But ...

VICTOR. That gives us four nights and three whole days.

OSCAR. This is ridiculous.

VICTOR. (*Goes very close to him and presses the gun against his chest.*) I have to tell you, Mr. Anderson. For me it is nothing new to kill a man. And one publisher more or less. What difference?

OSCAR. (*Terrified.*) Of course. But ... if you've got a novel, and I'm sure it's very good, why don't you get an agent?

VICTOR. Don't think I haven't tried. But three thousand pages, Mr. Anderson. It's a lot to read. Who will read them except at the point of a gun?

OSCAR. (*Losing his cool.*) So, put a gun to an *agent's* head. I can give you some addresses.

VICTOR. Then what? The agent puts a gun to a publisher's? This way I save time—and bullets.

OSCAR. (*Plaintively.*) But why *me*? There are a hundred publishers in London. What have *I* done, for Christ's sake?

VICTOR. Why *not* you? Anderson. It's the first name in the publishers' directory. What's the time?

OSCAR. It's almost six.

VICTOR. First we'll phone your wife. Then we'll settle down to work.

OSCAR. (*Making a last stand.*) Why can't you come back on Tuesday? I'll read it then. I promise.

VICTOR. (*Laughing and nodding to the phone.*) Your wife. She'll be expecting you home.

OSCAR. I have to think. I have to think. It's preposterous.

VICTOR. (*Raising the gun and picking up the phone.*) Shall I dial the number?

OSCAR. (*Grabs the receiver, dials, and waits, trembling. Into the phone.*) Harriet? Darling. Something awful. I've got to get to Paris tonight. Savarin's just phoned. Boudin's leaving in the morning. I've got to see him before he goes. Otherwise next week I'll have to go to New York.

VICTOR. Good. Good. Very good.

OSCAR. No, dear. No one's here. I'm sorry. (*Almost in tears.*) Yes, I'm alright. Of course I'm alright. I'm so sorry about tonight. It's just a confounded nuisance. No, I won't have time to get home. The plane leaves in a couple of hours.

VICTOR. Good, good.

OSCAR. I'll borrow some pyjamas from Savarin.

VICTOR. Better and better.

OSCAR. Darling, I'm so sorry. I'll see you Monday night.

VICTOR. Tuesday.

OSCAR. Or Tuesday. I know it sounds crazy, but I'm in a crazy business.

VICTOR. You can say that again.

OSCAR. Goodbye darling. (*HE puts the phone down and his head in his hands.*) This isn't happening to me. I'm dreaming.

VICTOR. (*Crosses to a cupboard, opens some doors until HE finds the drink.*) Here. Have a drink. You'll feel better. I'll join you. (*HE pours two drinks.*)

OSCAR. (*Heavy sarcasm.*) Help yourself. Make yourself at home.

VICTOR. (*The gun levelled.*) Listen. You and I are going to have to spend a long weekend together. You can accept it or fight it. But if you fight it, you can't win. So you might as well accept it with grace.

OSCAR. Give me some ice. There's a fridge in the corner.

VICTOR. (*Does and returns the glass.*) Shall we get started right away then? Or d'you want to eat first? I've brought a hamper.

OSCAR. You thought of everything, didn't you.

VICTOR. Well d'you want to eat or not?

OSCAR. Eat? I'd choke.

VICTOR. Then we'll get started.

OSCAR. This is crazy. (*Pause.*) All right. Pass it over.

VICTOR. That's not the plan. *I'm* going to read it, and you're going to listen.

OSCAR. But that's *real* crazy. It'll take twice as long.

VICTOR. It needs to be read aloud. Declaimed.

OSCAR. (*Angry.*) Why don't you go on the stage if it's an ego-trip you're after? God. Writers! (*With resolution.*) No. This is impossible. If I've got to read it, I've got to read it myself.

(VICTOR levels the gun once more.)

OSCAR. Alright. Alright. For God's sake get started. What's it called?

VICTOR. "A lesson in how not to conduct your life, even though you may be tempted and teased and promised great rewards, for there is a heavy price to pay for succumbing to temptation. For the body rebels and ages and sears before its time."

OSCAR. That's the *title*? Or the first chapter. (*Pause.*) It won't go on a jacket. *Any* jacket. Not even an Atlas jacket. Oh this is madness.

VICTOR. D'you want to start or don't you?

OSCAR. (*Shouting.*) Well to be frank with you, I don't want to start. Ever. I don't want to read, much less listen, to one lousy word of your novel. (*Pause.*) But I don't seem to have much choice.

VICTOR. That's better. Then I'll begin. I have to tell you first something about its setting and also ...

OSCAR. Stop. Now *you* stop and listen. D'you intend to approach every old lady who takes your book out of a library—should it ever get there—and should she be able to lift it—and say, "Now listen missus, before you read it, I have to tell you something about it's setting." If you've got to explain your book *before* you read it, you're probably written a bloody lousy novel.

VICTOR. You finished? I don't have to explain anything. I just wanted to put you in the mood.

OSCAR. (*Shouting.*) You'll never get me in the mood.

VICTOR. (*Also shouting.*) Well I'm going to give it a try. It's about this old man. Albert Smith he's called.

OSCAR. Oh, *very* original. What does he do, this Albert Smith?

VICTOR. He's a dentist.

OSCAR. That figures too.

VICTOR. But he's retired now. He's very old and he's looking back on his life.

OSCAR. Flashbacks, God help us. How old is he?

VICTOR. One hundred and two.

OSCAR. A hundred and two years of flashback. (*HE winces.*)

VICTOR. Not always years. Sometimes months. Even days.

OSCAR. Jesus, we'll be here forever.

VICTOR. Well settle down and I'll make a start. You ready?

OSCAR. (*Resigned.*) As ready as I'll ever be.

VICTOR. I'm not going to start reading if you're hostile. It's not fair on me. It doesn't give my work a chance.

OSCAR. (*Wryly.*) Oh I'm so sorry. I'm not hostile. I'm agog with excitement. I hang on your every syllable. (*Pause.*) Get on with it for Christ's sake.

VICTOR. O.K. Here we go. (*Declaiming.*) "Old age is not a blessing; it is simply a reward for having looked both ways before crossing the road." (*Pause. Looks up at Oscar.*) Not bad for openers, eh?

OSCAR. (*Impressed but careful to hide it.*) Listen, are you going stop after every sentence with your own comments?

VICTOR. I might. I might even repeat some sentences. Even paragraphs.

OSCAR. Oh goody. This is really going to be some weekend. (*Pause.*) Yes, it's a good beginning. Let's get to the end.

VICTOR. (*Reading.*) "… simply a reward for having looked both ways before crossing the road. Such were Albert Smith's thoughts as he sat at the lattice window of the Twilight Home for the elderly, and watched the ducks as they paddled in the pond in the garden outside."

(*The LIGHTS begin to dim very slowly as they do so, VICTOR's voice drones on in words that are unintelligible and barely audible. After a paragraph or two in the half dark:*)

OSCAR. (*Plaintively.*) I can't keep my eyes open. I've got to get some sleep.

VICTOR. O.K. I'll give you an hour, then I'll wake you with some coffee.

OSCAR. (*Wryly.*) So kind of you. (*Pause.*) I've got to go out for a pee.

VICTOR. I'm afraid I'm going to have to escort you. Can't take any chances.

OSCAR. Be my guest. (*Pause.*) I don't suppose you ever pee.

(*VICTOR puts the gun in Oscar's back. THEY go to the door and exit.*
LIGHTS dim completely.)

Scene 2

Saturday.
The scene as before. Part of Oscar's desk has been cleared to accommodate a coffee thermos and rolls. OSCAR looks like hell, but VICTOR is sprightly.

VICTOR. I hate to remind you, but you've got a phone call to make.

OSCAR. (*Half asleep.*) A phone call?

VICTOR. The airport.

OSCAR. Oh God. Deborah. (*Pause.*) What am I going to say? Poor sweetheart. What's the time?

VICTOR. 8:20. She'll be there by now.

OSCAR. I can't do it.

VICTOR. You've got to send some kind of message.

OSCAR. (*Shouting.*) But what, for Christ's sake?

VICTOR. D'you want me to do it for you?

OSCAR. (*Giving up.*) Would you?

VICTOR. (*Dials the number with some authority. Into phone.*) Air France desk please. (*Pause.*) My name is Oscar Anderson and I wish to leave a message for Deborah ... (*Whisper to Oscar.*) Deborah what?

OSCAR. Wooland.

(While VICTOR is talking, OSCAR hides himself, one ear cocked, eyes tight shut.)

VICTOR. *(Into phone.)* Miss Deborah Wooland. She's waiting to board the Air France flight to Paris. I need to get a message to her most urgently. Oscar Anderson. *(Pause.)* Tell her that I cannot get to Paris this weekend. I cannot be contacted. I'll explain everything on Tuesday. *(Pause.)* Oh, and tell her I'm very sorry.

OSCAR. *(Genuinely, with feeling.)* Thank you. I'm deeply grateful. *(Pause, shouting.)* What the hell am I grateful for? You've landed me in this shit and I'm *thanking* you for it. This is crazy.

VICTOR. Have some more coffee. *(Tucks his gun under his arm, and pours some coffee. Then HE cocks it and passes the coffee to Oscar.)*

VICTOR. Shall I get started?

OSCAR. *(Irritated.)* Well I can't go home and I can't go to Paris. There's nothing I *can* do but stay here. So you might as well get on with it. And do me a favour. Put that gun away. It makes me nervous.

VICTOR. Alright. But don't try anything.

OSCAR. Like what? You got any ideas?

VICTOR. *(Picking up manuscript.)* I'm going to go from where we left off. You ready?

OSCAR. What page are we on?

VICTOR. Three hundred and six.

OSCAR. Three hundred and six? That's already longer than a normal novel. Three hundred and six pages and we're still on the introduction. When is something going to *happen*? An *event*. A *plot*. Three hundred and six pages of a boring old codger reminiscing about his sexual philanderings. But in *theory*. Three hundred and six pages of theory. He sits there and speculates, and all that's possibly *happened* is a severe case of piles. For God's sake, when does the old bugger get up off his arse and get moving?

VICTOR. Funny you should mention it. He does. This very chapter. Chapter eleven. You ready?

(OSCAR nods wearily.)

VICTOR. *(Reading.)* "Yes, Albert thought to himself. A man can adulterate only once. Any subsequent filing is infidelity." *(Looking up.)* D'you like that? Shall I read it again?

OSCAR. No. Yes, I do like it, but no, don't read it again. *(Aside.)* Not true, anyway.

VICTOR. *(Reading.)* "He thought of that first time, that very first trespass against his marriage vows. Isabel had been his wife for five years. Poor Isabel. He could not bear to think of it. With infinite care, he rose from his seat."

OSCAR. *(Yelling.)* EUREKA! Albert Smith has risen! Mark that page. An event! A happening! A hint maybe, a soupçon of a plot.

VICTOR. *(Ignoring him. Reading.)* "And slowly he padded around his room, tapping his stick, blinding his past." *(To Oscar.)* Perhaps I should re-write that phrase. Make it clearer.

OSCAR. NO. It's infinitely clear. Get on with it for heaven sake. I'm terrified old Albert might sit down again. Stay on your doddering feet, Bertie, I beg of you.

(The LIGHTS on the office begin to dim, and come up on insert stage. The sole prop a double bed and bedside lamp attached. A mattress and a blanket. No more. On it lies HARRIET (now ISABEL) dressed and dishevelled. Over this:)

VICTOR. (V.O.) "… tapping his stick, blinding his past. He hoped that the concentration required to steer his body around the room would leave no space in his mind for thoughts of that terrible morning of poor Isabel's discovery. Coming home late was one thing. Staying out all night was quite another."

(ISABEL is restless. The sound of a DOOR opening. SHE sits up and listens. FOOTSTEPS. Another DOOR. FLUSH of loo. Enter OSCAR (now ALBERT). A wig covers the erstwhile bald patch. Undressed, HE tip-toes towards the bed. ISABEL switches on the lamp. The inset stage is flooded with LIGHT.)

ALBERT. (*Frightened.*) What you do that for? Stupid thing to do.
ISABEL. (*Flabbergasted.*) Do what? Listen, before you start turning tables …
ALBERT. (*Last stand.*) Well it was a bloody silly thing to do to put the light on. Insensitive.
ISABEL. Ha. That's a good word coming from you.
ALBERT. Put it out.

ISABEL. No. I want to *see* what you're saying. I want to see your answer. Where have you been? (*Pause, then shouting.*) I *know* you've been with Carol.

ALBERT. (*Quietly.*) Then why do you ask?

ISABEL. (*Control.*) I can't take it any more. All your lies. All your excuses. All your pleas to give you time to make up your mind. I've given you time. Three years of Carol time. Now it's too late for discussion.

ALBERT. What d'you mean?

ISABEL. It's ultimatum time.

ALBERT. That's fish-wife stuff. That's not you, Isabel.

ISABEL. No? Don't kid yourself. This *is* me. If three years ago I'd written to any agony aunt for advice, they would have suggested ultimatum. But we're much too intelligent for that kind of stuff, aren't we? We weigh up all the issues. We throttle ourselves with decency and understanding. Well I tell you, I've been so bloody decent and intelligent these last three years, I make myself sick. So now it's fish-wife stuff, Albert, whether you like it or not.

ALBERT. Isabel ... I need ... time to work it all out. I need time to find myself.

ISABEL. (*Laughing.*) What happens to me while you're finding yourself? No, I'll spell it out for you Albert. Me or her.

ALBERT. (*Helplessly.*) What d'you want me to say?

ISABEL. I'll tell you the truth. I hope it's her. Because if it were me, you'd punish me for the rest of my life. I don't want to be the choice of no choice at all. So I'll do the choosing. Get out. And now. No talk, no pleading, no time-begging. No sentiment. No nostalgia. None of your maudlin devices.

VICTOR. (*V.O., with deliberation, word for word.*) Isabel—said—angrily.

OSCAR. (*Shouting to Victor.*) Oh shut up. I can't cope with you too.

ALBERT. *Please* Isabel, give me time.

ISABEL. (*Losing her cool.*) Get out. If I hear that phrase again, I'll go mad. You're like a cuckoo coming out of a clock, begging for what you've taken anyway. Time. Joke is, I'm the cuckoo.

ALBERT. Isabel ... you can't ... I mean ... this is ridiculous. You can't mean it.

ISABEL. Get out. This minute. And take your things. Whatever you'll leave, I'll throw out.

(*LIGHTS on inset stage dim.*)

VICTOR. (*V.O. Reading.*) "So Albert had no choice. He packed what he could but not very seriously because he did not for one moment believe that Isabel was in earnest."

OSCAR. (*Comes out on to apron stage and takes off his wig.*) No. It's all wrong, Victor. Isabel would not have said that. She knows that ultimatum is the last card that she can play. Once that's gone, it's all over. Albert keeps asking for time and Isabel is frightened of not giving it. That way they live happily ever after.

VICTOR. You've got yourself a doormat there. And Deborah's another one. You've really fixed it up nicely for yourself, haven't you?

OSCAR. How dare you! (*HE goes for him.*)

HARRIET. (*Comes out of inset stage. SHE tries to separate them.*) Stop it.

OSCAR. Get out of my life. My wife and I are very happy.

VICTOR. (*Laughing.*) Not in my book.

HARRIET. You don't understand, do you. Oscar's right. God help me but he's right. There *is* a kind of happiness. I understand him.

VICTOR. That kind of understanding is crippling. He exploits it.

HARRIET. Yes I know. I'm well aware of that. But it's *my* choice. I have the *nerve* to understand him. I have the decency. And my decency gets on his nerves. That's why he goes to other women. And I *let* him. That's what it's all about. *Collusion.*

OSCAR. (*Weakly in the middle of them.*) Well ... it's ...er ... not exactly like ...

VICTOR. (*With contempt.*) Look at you. Bursting at the seams with indecision. You're weak, and a bully to beat.

HARRIET. Leave him alone. (*SHE goes to put her arms around Oscar. Almost in tears.*) Why is he interfering with us Oscar?

OSCAR. (*Protectively.*) Don't cry, darling. We'll be alright.

VICTOR. (*Impatient.*) Listen, this is *my* novel and the kind of women I write about are those who take a stand.

HARRIET. Well I can't play that role with any conviction.

VICTOR. Well it's about time you tried. And take it from me, you're not doing too badly.

OSCAR. Leave my wife alone. Don't you start putting ideas into her head. (*Angry.*) What do you writers care?

We're just copy for you. And when you've written it, you just bugger off and leave us with the pieces.

HARRIET. You're no better than Deborah and her kind. You're a parasite. You batten off other people's lives. If anyone's a cuckoo, you are.

VICTOR. (*To Oscar.*) Put your wig back on. (*HE raises the gun.*)

OSCAR. O.K. O.K. I'll get my cases.

(*Exit ISABEL and OSCAR into inset stage.*
After a beat, ALBERT comes out front carrying a half-open suitcase with clothes hanging out. A pair of shoes thrown from behind, narrowly misses his head. ALBERT kneels and stuffs the case closed.
Enter mime taxi, its "hire" light shining. VICTOR is the driver. ALBERT waves frantically. The cab slows down.)

ALBERT. 22, Salisbury Mount. (*HE climbs on Victor's back.*) Haven't we met before?

CABBIE. (*Jewish East End.*) An hour ago I picked you up already. From the same address you're going to. Busy, busy. (*HE drives off.*) Such a nice morning.

ALBERT. Depends on how you feel.

CABBIE. So feel good. What you running back and fore?

ALBERT. I don't see it's any of your business.

CABBIE. (*Laughs.*) Your business is my business. Oops!

(*VICTOR swerves the cab and pulls up at the inset stage. ALBERT alights and pays the fare.*

LIGHT on bed. DEBORAH (now CAROL) is dressing.
Enter ALBERT.)

CAROL. Albert, what are you doing here?

ALBERT. (*Nonchalant.*) Oh … I thought I'd come back … Take another look at you.

CAROL. With your suitcase?

ALBERT. I … have to take some things to the dry cleaners.

CAROL. She threw you out.

ALBERT. Don't talk rubbish. I just thought …

CAROL. Albert, she threw you out. And you came here. (*Pause.*) And you're not going back.

ALBERT. (*Shouting.*) Of course I'm going back.

CAROL. Then she did throw you out.

ALBERT. No she didn't. I left.

(CAROL crosses over and fondles him as:)

VICTOR. (*V.O., reading.*) "Well of course it's only a question of semantics. Who leaves whom. 'A' gives a little push and 'B' leaves. You don't go unless you've been pushed. So who leaves whom? No one is to blame. Everyone colludes. So no one is guilty."

OSCAR. (*Pokes his head out of inset stage. Shouting.*) I like that bit, Victor. It's really not a bad novel at all.

VICTOR. Get on with your part.

OSCAR. Gratitude!

CAROL. Are you staying with me then?

ALBERT. I need time. I've got to think things over. Oh it's all such a mess.

CAROL. It doesn't have to be. All it takes is just one decision. We've been together for three years. It's more than enough to make up one's mind. You've got it good, you know. You've got two women who are prepared to give you time. Why *should* you make a decision?

ALBERT. Let's go to bed.

CAROL. We know that works. That won't solve anything.

ALBERT. But I need *comfort*. Come on sweetheart.

(Half undressed THEY get onto the bed, covering themselves with a blanket. An attempt at discreet love-making. Clearly frustrated, ALBERT distances himself from Carol and lies on his back.)

VICTOR. *(Watching, and over the above.)* Poor Oscar's not going to like this bit at all. Well what does he expect, the fool. *(Reading.)* "Poor Albert. Like all men he didn't understand the notion of cause and effect."

OSCAR. *(Shouting.)* Rubbish.

CAROL. What's the matter, Albert?

ALBERT. I don't know. Something's happened.

VICTOR. *(V.O., reading.)* "Or more to the point, something *hasn't* happened."

CAROL. Be patient, darling. It'll be alright.

VICTOR. *(V.O., reading.)* "But it wasn't. And wouldn't be. Albert was running in a play that's a three-hander. If one player leaves the cast, there's no play any more. Poor Albert. His third party opted out. Mate in three was the name of the game. *Naughty* Isabel."

ALBERT. *(Rising from the bed.)* I've got to go.

CAROL. Where?

ALBERT. I'm going home. I can't leave her. Five years. Two children. I can't.

CAROL. So you've made a decision at last.

ALBERT. I need ... (*But even he is bored with saying it.*)

CAROL. (*Blowing.*) You've had time enough. Don't come here again. Ever. Ever. D'you hear?

(*ALBERT looks at her in astonishment. SHE suddenly clings to him.*)

CAROL. Oh I don't know why I said that. I'll never send you away. You know that. The words just ... just came out of my mouth ... as if they weren't my words at all.

VICTOR. (*Shouting.*) They weren't, because this is my novel. Now throw him out, d'you hear?

CAROL. (*Listlessly.*) Don't come here again. Ever, ever. D'you hear?

VICTOR. Go on. Throw out his clothes.

(*CAROL obeys, but plants his pants and jacket gently on the apron stage. ALBERT follows carrying his suitcase. Wearily HE dresses. After a beat, enter mime cab with VICTOR at the wheel. ALBERT flags him down.*)

ALBERT. D'you have the sole concession of this route?

CABBIE. I make a living. Back to the same address?

ALBERT. How do you know?

CABBIE. It's my business to know.

*(ALBERT nods, climbs in behind cabbie. THEY travel a
little, then stop.)*

   ALBERT. Why are we stopping?
   CABBIE. Red light. You in a hurry, sir?
   ALBERT. Er … no.
   CABBIE. What's to hurry, I ask myself. You miss a
train. Is another. Rush rush. Soon enough we're all dead.
So why hurry?

(The cab jerks away with a jolt.)

   CABBIE. Sorry, sir. Gear a bit unreliable. Like most
things these days. (*Pause.*) So we're here already.

(The cab pulls up. ALBERT alights and pays fare.)

   CABBIE. What d'you think? I should wait for you?
   ALBERT. (*Crossly.*) No. I shan't be needing you.
   CABBIE. (*Aside.*) Don't you be too sure. (*HE drives
off.*)

*(ALBERT mimes fumbling for his keys. HE hesitates.
Prepares to knock. Thinks better of it. Opens the door
with his key. There is a covered LUMP in the bed.
ALBERT touches it gingerly.)*

   ALBERT. (*Tenderly.*) Isabel?

*(The LUMP shifts but no head is raised. Carefully
ALBERT pulls down the blanket. VICTOR sits bolt
upright in bed.)*

ALBERT. What the hell are you doing here?

VICTOR. (*On his dignity.*) Why shouldn't I be here? It's *my* novel. I'm a teller of stories, a weaver of tales. I have some say in their design. I'm thickening the plot. (*Calling.*) Come dearest.

(ISABEL wafts towards the bed in her nightdress. ALBERT pulls her out of the inset stage.)

OSCAR. (*Infuriated.*) How can you let him into your bed? *Our* bed.

HARRIET. I'm part of his plot. I don't have much choice. I'm being used. That seems to be my role.

OSCAR. Why don't you stand up for yourself, for God's sake? Say *no*. Assert yourself a little. Er … no … don't do that. That'll only lead to trouble.

VICTOR. (*Shouting.*) You've got to go now Albert. You're not in this chapter.

OSCAR. (*Petulant.*) I'm not taking this book. I'm just not taking this book.

(HARRIET returns to inset stage. ALBERT squats down disconsolately outside.)

OSCAR. It's all wrong. It's not as cut and dried as all that. But if I don't let him thicken his plot, old Albert will sit down again, and I've had three hundred and six pages of that. So get weaving, you *author* you.

(Sounds of LOVE-MAKING from inset stage.)

ALBERT. Oh I can't bear it. (*HE picks up his case and starts walking. Calling.*) Taxi! (*HE watches as an imaginary cab drives past him.*) Pig! (*HE trudges on, then stops to talk. HE sits on his case.*) I don't understand it at all. What have I done? I can't make a decision. Is that such a sin? It's true I want the best of both worlds. Does that make me a criminal? It makes me a man, that's all. Women are different. I respect women. (*Another cab passes. Yelling with rage.*) Taxi! (*HE starts walking again.*) I adore women. I said that to Isabel once. And she said, yes, I know you do. But you don't *like* them. That's your trouble. I didn't know what she was talking about. I *do* adore women. But they're different. They're home-makers, nest-builders. Monogamous.

(*Shrieks of LAUGHTER from inset stage.*)

ALBERT. (*Angry.*) He's got it all wrong, that Victor. And what makes him think that Isabel would fancy him? God, they're so arrogant, these writers. (*HE trudges to the end of the apron, turns, and starts back again towards the bed. On the way rehearsing. Bonhomie.*) Hullo Carol. I've come back. I'm ... I'm staying. Yes. I'll stay with you. Alright. In *time* I'll marry you. (*Amending that.*) No, not marriage. I don't have to be that crazy. (*Calling timidly.*) Carol?

(*HE mimes opening the door with his key.*
CAROL is in bed.)

ALBERT. Darling, I'm back.

CAROL. (*Sitting up.*) I told you not to come. Anyway, I'm expecting somebody.

ALBERT. (*Spluttering.*) What? You don't lose much time.

CAROL. I meant what I said. (*Calling.*) I'm ready, darling.

(*Enter VICTOR in dressing-gown. HE makes to get into the bed.*)

ALBERT. (*To Carol.*) How can you do it?

CAROL. I'm a young woman. I'm not about to go into a nunnery because you can't make up your mind.

ALBERT. (*Going for Victor's throat.*) You bastard!

VICTOR. What's the matter with you, you maniac? When I slept with your wife you didn't lift a finger to stop me.

ALBERT. Wives are different.

VICTOR. Rubbish. That's *your* problem. You work it out. Now shove off. I've got to keep the plot going.

(*VICTOR pushes ALBERT out of the inset stage. ALBERT outside, dusts himself down.*)

ALBERT. What's happening to these women? They're behaving like men. It's not right. It's not natural. Huh, it's a joke. I paid 250,000 pounds for a house for me and Isabel, and a 100,000 for Carol's flat. All my sweat-earned money. And *I* don't have a place to sleep. (*Rising anger.*) Well it's crazy. They can't do this to me.

VICTOR. (*V.O.*) Finally it's money. It always comes down to money.

ALBERT. (*Blowing.*) Oh shut up!

(*LIGHTS come up slowly on publisher's office. OSCAR sits at his desk, drooping with fatigue. VICTOR is reading.*)

VICTOR. "But despite the sundry inconveniences of his life, despite the massive alimony, to say nothing of his settlement of breach of promise to Carol, poor Albert learned no lesson."

OSCAR. (*With contempt.*) Of course he didn't. Why should he? It wasn't *his* fault his women took him to the cleaners. Anyway, I'm dropping for sleep. What day is it?

VICTOR. Saturday. Midnight, Saturday.

OSCAR. God it feels like I've been here for years. What page are we on now?

VICTOR. Almost eight hundred.

OSCAR. Not even half way. Jesus. I'm tired.

VICTOR. Well you've had quite a busy day.

OSCAR. You've not been exactly idle yourself.

VICTOR. (*Pours Oscar a drink.*) Here, have a night cap. Then a short sleep. Then one more spurt to the half-way mark, and I'll give you a whole night. How's that?

OSCAR. You're too kind.

VICTOR. I'll join you I think. (*HE pours himself a drink.*) Cheers.

OSCAR. To what, for God's sake?

VICTOR. Oh anything.

(*Pause. OSCAR starts to drink.*)

VICTOR. To women.

(OSCAR fairly chokes.)

VICTOR. To your two children then. Tucked away in their boarding schools.

OSCAR. Is there anything you *don't* know about me?

VICTOR. Not much. But what there is, I'm learning.

(LIGHTS dim.)

Scene 3

Sunday.

As the LIGHTS come up on the publisher's office, VICTOR is heard reading, unintelligibly at first, and then with clarity as the LIGHTS brighten.

OSCAR sits at his desk gulping coffee, surrounded by rolls, butter, and a jar of marmalade.

VICTOR. *(Reading.)* "But despite the sundry inconveniences of his life, despite the massive alimony ..."

OSCAR. You read that bit already.

VICTOR. I'm putting you back in the picture.

(OSCAR raises his eyes to the ceiling.)

VICTOR. *(Reading.)* "Poor Albert learnt no lesson. He married again, and shortly afterwards he took a mistress, as if the one were a corollary of the other. But Doris was not like Carol. She lacked Carol's refinement, and, unlike

Carol, she was not given to martyrdom. One night, in a fit of fury at Albert's inability to make a choice, she told him he ought to go and get himself seen to. (*Rises.*) Come on Oscar, I need your help in this chapter.

OSCAR. It had to come some time or another, didn't it. What d'you want me to do?

VICTOR. Nothing. Just work this hair dryer, and keep your mouth shut.

OSCAR. Charming.

(*LIGHTS dim and come up on inset stage. Two empty chairs face the audience. VICTOR takes another hair dryer from a box, and with a springy hairdresser's step, HE positions himself behind one of the chairs. OSCAR follows without appetite.*)

OSCAR. What d'you want me to do?

VICTOR. Stand here (*HE places him behind the second chair.*) and blow-dry the next client.

OSCAR. Blow-dry?

VICTOR. (*Impatient.*) Oh just blow. (*Calling.*) Mrs. Smith?

OSCAR. Oh God no.

(*Enter HARRIET (now MARY). SHE sits herself at Oscar's stand.*)

VICTOR. (*To Oscar.*) Get going.

(*VICTOR turns on the dryer for him. OSCAR is at a loss, but does his amateur best.*)

VICTOR. Jesus. Watch me. (*HE uses the dryer then hands it over. Calling.*) Miss Brown?

(*Enter DEBORAH (now DORIS). SHE sits at Victor's stand.*)

OSCAR. (*Almost in tears.*) This isn't fair. (*To Victor.*) You bastard.

(*Throughout this scene, VICTOR uses the hand-dryer as a baton, conducting the dialogue and bringing in each actress on cue. Often HE mouths the words along with them, and with affected facial expressions. The dryers BUZZ loudly.*)

DORIS. (*Cockney and yelling above the dryer.*) So I said to 'im, Bert, I said, you ought to go and 'ave yerself seen to. (*SHE turns to Victor and shouts.*) Listen.

(*VICTOR shuts off the dryers.*)

DORIS. I'm not talking like that. It's not my style. That's just a stereotyped whore who's taken a man whose wife doesn't understand him. That's not me at all.
VICTOR. This is my novel and you'll do as I say.
DORIS. You don't like women very much, do you?
OSCAR. (*Laughing.*) Does this happen with all your novels?
VICTOR. (*Shouting to Doris.*) You're cockney, d'you hear? A cockney tart.
DORIS. (*Wide cockney.*) 'Ave it yer own way, cock. (*Aside.*) Damn silly way too.

VICTOR. (*Yelling.*) I know I'm right.

DORIS. You're not short on certainty, are you, (*Pause.*) cock?

VICTOR. Get going. (*HE turns on the dryer.*)

DORIS. So I said to 'im, Bert, I said, you ought to go and 'ave yerself seen to. You saying I'm balmy, 'e said. No, I said to 'im, but you ought to go to a psychiatrist. They're all the rage now, I said.

OSCAR. Oh Doris, shut up. *Please.*

(*MARY is too refined to raise her voice in response, so SHE smiles.*)

DORIS. Come 'ere often, do you.

(*MARY shakes her head.*)

DORIS. Neither do I. Can't afford it. But Bert's paying. My name's Doris. What's yours?

(*MARY mouths "Mary."*)

DORIS. Mary, is it?

(*MARY nods.*)

DORIS. I'm going to Paris tonight, Mary.

OSCAR. Oh my God.

DORIS. Gay Paree. Old Bert's taking me. Told 'is wife 'e's going to a conference. (*Laughs.*) Oh 'e's a cunning devil, old Bert. She believes 'im too.

OSCAR. Silly bitch.

MARY. (*Moment of shock on Mary's face.*) What does he do, this … er … Bert of yours.
DORIS. (*Yelling.*) What? Can't hear you.

(*MARY tucks her head under Doris' flying hair and speaks into her ear.*)

DORIS. Bert? My Albert's a dentist.
MARY. I'll kill you.

(*SHE makes to throttle Doris. OSCAR intervenes. HE puts his arm round Mary's shoulder.*)

OSCAR. Darling, please. In the end it's you who matters.

(*THEY hold each other as the LIGHTS dim and come up on the office.*)

OSCAR. That's the last time I'm helping you on any chapter.
VICTOR. I had to have someone to hold the other dryer. I couldn't have conducted otherwise.
OSCAR. Writers, God help me. (*Pause.*) Let's get on with it.

(*THEY both settle at their desks.*)

VICTOR. (*Reading.*) "Poor Albert. Another divorce. Another breach of promise. More alimony. More settlement. So finally, though by now he hated her, he took Doris' advice. He decided to go and get himself seen to. But he was frightened. He didn't want his secrets known. He didn't want his frailty exposed. He was ashamed of his weakness, and he was ashamed of his shame."

OSCAR. (*Fearful.*) I'm tired. I've got to get some more sleep.

VICTOR. Only another dozen pages and then we're half way.

OSCAR. I can't.

(LIGHTS begin to dim over the office.)

VICTOR. You must, otherwise we won't get finished.

OSCAR. (*Angry.*) I don't want to. Leave me alone.

VICTOR. Come on now. It's for your own good.

(LIGHTS up on stage inset. VICTOR as PSYCHIATRIST sits in a chair. ALBERT lies on a couch.
A portrait of Freud on the wall.)

ALBERT. You don't mind, Doctor, if I go to sleep?

DOCTOR. (*German accent.*) Who am I to mind? But ... but but but, it is a very expensive sleep you have. Forty pounds for forty winks. An expensive wink. Already you've had five. Why not first tell me why you have come. And afterwards, perhaps, a little sleep.

ALBERT. Can't I sleep first and then tell you?

DOCTOR. You should sleep in *your* time. *Your* time is cheaper.

ALBERT. (*Sits bolt upright. Roused.*) Cheaper? D'you you know what I earn in an hour, Doctor? I'm not on the National Health you know. I'm in private practice. D'you know what I charge for a bridge? Two hundred fifty pounds.

And that's the smallest one. A bigger one, that stretches over more teeth—well, anything up to a thousand.

DOCTOR. Tell me about these bridges of yours.

ALBERT. A bridge is a work of art you know, Doctor. Anyone could make a bridge. Even you could make a bridge. Like anyone could paint a painting or write a novel. *Especially* a novel. But there are good bridges and bad bridges. Only an artist can make a good bridge.

DOCTOR. Tell me about it.

ALBERT. (*Laughing.*) I'm paying you and you're asking for lessons on how to make a bridge. It's you should be giving *me* lessons.

DOCTOR. Lessons in what?

ALBERT. (*Quickly.*) I'll tell you how to make a bridge. It can't do any harm.

(During the course of his speech, ALBERT uses the DOCTOR as his patient, forcing his mouth open and maneuvering inside it with a hint of happy vengeance.)

ALBERT. Now supposing say, you need a bridge between the first molar and the last canine. Just here. First I have to ascertain that the roots of the supporting teeth are healthy. This I have to do with x-rays. Open wide. Then I have to take an impression. For the bite. Then I have to decide whether you want gold on the outside as well as on the inside. I leave that to you to decide, the patient, and I can tell a lot about him from his choice.

DOCTOR. (*Takes Albert's hands away from his mouth.*) You love your work don't you, Mr. Smith.

ALBERT. Yes, I do.

DOCTOR. D'you know what I felt then when you were fitting my bridge? I felt you had power over me. Did you feel that?

ALBERT. Oh yes, well you see, a dentist does. I can stuff your mouth with cotton wool and then I can say anything to you. Anything at all. I can insult you, I can malign you, I can slander you, and you cannot answer back.

DOCTOR. You like that, eh? And what about when you are not in your surgery? How do you—how d'you say—exercise your power? (*No pause.*) You're married, Mr. Smith?

ALBERT. What's that got to do with anything?

DOCTOR. Probably nothing. I'm very interested in you. Your life. I've not talked so long to a dentist before.

ALBERT. I'm divorced. (*Pause.*) Twice.

DOCTOR. (*Laughing.*) Couldn't stuff their mouths with cotton wool.

ALBERT. (*Laughs for want of any alternative.*) Tried.

DOCTOR. Had minds of their own, eh?

(*Pause.*)

ALBERT. (*Looking at him.*) You know Doctor, you could use a little orthodonty.

DOCTOR. (*Laughing.*) I couldn't afford you.

ALBERT. We could ... er ... make a deal?

DOCTOR. Mr. Smith, if you want to insult me, go ahead. Insult. Not necessary for me to be in your chair. But you didn't come here for that. I know. Why did you come?

ALBERT. Doris said I ought to.

DOCTOR. Tell me about Doris.

ALBERT. I'm not paying out good money just to tell you about Doris. She's not worth a penny a syllable.

(Pause.)

DOCTOR. How have women hurt you?

ALBERT. You know Doctor, presuming you've got all your teeth. I would have to cap every one of them, three times over before you'd earn enough to get the answer to that question.

DOCTOR. I have to tell you Mr. Smith, as you've probably already noticed, my teeth are in excellent condition.

ALBERT. Then I'm sorry Doctor, I can do no more for you. (*HE rises.*) But you owe me. Apart from the lesson in bridgework, I've also paid you a fee. D'you have nothing to tell me? No advice to give?

DOCTOR. On what? First you have to tell me why you came.

ALBERT. Don't you *know*? I've been talking to you for the last hour and you don't *know*?

DOCTOR. I know enough to know one thing. Whatever advice I should give you, you wouldn't take it. You don't want it. Your coming here was only a gesture. You don't want to change yourself.

ALBERT. For that you went to University? Good day, Doctor.

(LIGHTS dim on inset stage and LIGHT on publisher's office.)

VICTOR. (*Reading.*) "The doctor was right. Albert didn't want to change. And as long as there were women like Isabel, Carol, Mary and Doris around, and countless other corpses that littered his wayside, he didn't have to."

OSCAR. (*At desk.*) The doctor wasn't right. I hope he isn't typical of his profession. He said nothing, absolutely nothing and got paid for it.

VICTOR. He said to Albert, "How have women hurt you?" That's a key question.

OSCAR. Not in my ... Albert's case. He adored women.

VICTOR. That's the whole point. Like Isabel said in the beginning. He adored them but he didn't *like* them. He either put them on a pedestal or underneath one. In fact he hated them. He punished them coitally, one by one. Oh yes, he adored them, but to adore is to be afraid, and from fear springs hatred.

OSCAR. You should be a psychiatrist.

VICTOR. I am. All novelists are. Or should be.

OSCAR. Well, I tell you, you'd make a better living out of shrinking than you ever will out of a novel.

VICTOR. There's just one more page to go. Then we're half way.

OSCAR. Go ahead.

VICTOR. "Albert shuffled back to the window. He shifted his chair into the light of the setting sun, and he sat down."

OSCAR. No! For God's sake, he can't sit down again.

VICTOR. Listen, he's an old man of one hundred and two. He's got to sit down. Or he'll just die of exhaustion.

OSCAR. That's another reason for keeping him on his feet.

VICTOR. (*Reading, ignoring him.*) "… in the light of the setting sun, and sat down."

OSCAR. Does that mean another three hundred pages of interior monologue?

VICTOR. He's just resting. Like you and me are going to rest.

OSCAR. Thank God. (*Pause.*) What day is it?

VICTOR. It's almost Monday. 11:30. (*To himself, counting on his fingers.*) 10, 9, 8, 7, … Can I use your phone?

OSCAR. (*Tired.*) Be my guest.

(*VICTOR crosses over to Oscar's desk, picks up the phone. HE dials an inordinate amount of numbers that seem to go on for ever. OSCAR boggles.*)

OSCAR. Where the hell are you dialling?

VICTOR. Sydney, Australia. Lots of numbers. But cheaper with direct dial. Cheap rate too. It's Sunday. My wife. (*Pause.*) I hope her mother doesn't answer the phone.

OSCAR. What's she doing there, your wife?

VICTOR. She left me. (*Pause.*) It's ringing.

OSCAR. Good for her. I wish I could do the same.

VICTOR. Shit! It's her mother. Hullo? Mrs. Johnson? It's Victor. Can I speak to Brenda? (*Pause.*) I'm in London. (*Shouting.*) Well go and ask her. Let her come to the phone and tell me to my face that she doesn't want to speak to me. (*Pause.*) Hurry up. (*To Oscar.*) She's gone to fetch her.

OSCAR. You mean you're phoning Australia, and holding *on*? And on *my* telephone?

VICTOR. She won't be long. I can hear them arguing.
Hullo? (*Yelling.*) Hullo. Come to the phone.

(*Pause while OSCAR and VICTOR nervously stare at each
    other.*)

VICTOR. (*Shouting.*) Hullo? (*To Oscar.*) I'll kill her.
OSCAR. Put it down. She's not coming. (*Pause.*) Put
it *down*. (*HE grabs the phone and puts it down.*)
VICTOR. She would have come. I bet she's picked up
the phone by now.
OSCAR. You bet she hasn't. You'd still be hanging
on. It would be cheaper to fly out to Sydney and talk to
her. Even if she doesn't listen. (*Pause.*) Why did she leave
you?
VICTOR. I had an affair. A long affair.
OSCAR. Ha! That's a joke. And you judge Albert.
VICTOR. Not for his adultery. Albert is a non-
committing man. That's why I judge him.
OSCAR. And you are? Committed, I mean. Whatever
anyone means by that word.
VICTOR. I had an affair with a novel. The one we're
reading. I committed adultery with fiction, and that's more
unforgivable than the other kind. My wife was real and not
half as much fun. (*Pause.*) Listen, perhaps *you* could talk
to her.
OSCAR. I have a small sense that the roles are
reversing. No, of course I can't talk to her. Especially over
six thousand miles. You know heart-to-hearts. They're not
talking. They're pauses, sighs, sobs and uninterruptable
tears. At a pound a minute, you'd be better off getting a
divorce and paying the alimony. (*Pause.*) Come on Victor,

you're feeling badly because you've finished the novel. It's like the end of an affair. It's always depressing. You can write another. Maybe if it's not so long, she'd tolerate it. Look—I've really got to get some sleep.

VICTOR. I've got to call her back. At least leave a message. Please. I'll give you back the money.

OSCAR. I'm too tired to deny you. But make it quick. (*HE goes to the couch and lies down.*)

VICTOR. (*Dials and waits. Resolute.*) Hullo? Mrs. Johnson? I want to leave a message for my wife. Tell her to ring me at 636-6624. In London. You got that? Tell her to call collect.

(*OSCAR shoots up from the couch.*)

VICTOR. Tell her. Or there'll be trouble.

(*HE replaces the receiver. OSCAR splutters.*)

VICTOR. Don't worry. I'll pay. (*HE pours himself another drink.To Oscar.*) Want one?

OSCAR. Why the hell not?

(*HE passes a glass to Oscar then sits by his side on the couch, holding the bottle. HE replenishes their glasses during their conversation, and BOTH get progressively drunker.*)

VICTOR. Women! I don't know Oscar, what's more important to you. Women or your work?

OSCAR. Oh I don't know. I've never thought about it.

VICTOR. For me it's work. It's the only thing that's reliable.

OSCAR. What's so good about reliable? My tailor's reliable. So is the arrival of my gas bill. There's no virtue in reliability. It's what's *unknown, unpredictable* that makes life exciting. It's taking risks.

VICTOR. And what d'you think a writer does every time he picks up his pen? But you've got to be committed to what you're doing. Just in one area. You can't spread yourself.

OSCAR. Why d'you keep on bleating about commitment? What the hell does that word mean? Is it only applied to work? Am I a committed publisher? Is there such a thing as a committed tobacconist? Listen, Albert Smith is not a non-committing man. All he is is selfish. He's mean, and he wants everything this own way. And to that end he *uses* people. Most of all women. He takes advantage of their frailties. He's ... a ... pig.

VICTOR. (*Laughing.*) You think so. I'm more generous than you. I think he's weak, that's all.

OSCAR. Where's there the law that says men have got to be strong? Where's the law that says we've got to be more intelligent? Those laws are made by women's expectations. And if we don't live up to them we're branded. (*Laughs.*) You know Victor, my old fruit, you really get on my nerves. You've ruined my weekend, you're deafening me with your prose. You're costing me a fortune in telephone bills—yet—you've got something. I don't know what it is but you've got something.

VICTOR. (*Laughing.*) Well, if I look hard enough, very hard mind you, I reckon you've got something too.

OSCAR. One more for the road.

VICTOR. I'll join you.

(THEY drain their glasses then OSCAR lies down on the couch.)

OSCAR. Jesus, I'm tired.
VICTOR. Shove over. (*HE settles himself beside Oscar on the couch.*) And the lion shall lie down with the lamb.

(As the LIGHTS dim:)

VICTOR. Or vice versa.

ACT II

Scene 1

Monday.
VICTOR is pouring the coffee at his desk.
OSCAR still snores on the couch.
VICTOR crosses over to Oscar with a cup of coffee. HE puts it down on his desk and gently shakes him.

VICTOR. Wake up. It's nine o'clock.

OSCAR. (*Sleeping.*) Deborah? (*Waking.*) Oh it's you. Leave me alone. (*HE turns over.*)

VICTOR. (*Shakes him again.*) We've got to get started.

OSCAR. (*Slowly rising.*) *You've* got to get started maybe. As I remember, old Albert has sat down again, and from past experience I know I can safely go back to sleep until he stands up.'Cos nothing, absolutely nothing, is going to happen.

VICTOR. You're wrong. *Age* happens. That's not an event? Invisible maybe. Predictable too. But it's a happening.

OSCAR. Oh you're so depressing.

VICTOR. It's a happening you don't notice. Or you choose to ignore. But it nudges you. It lames your step. It plays tricks on your body, thins your hair, etches lines into your face.

OSCAR. Oh shut up, for God's sake. Where's that coffee?

VICTOR. (*Hands him his cup.*) Want a roll?
Marmalade? Hard-boiled egg?

(*OSCAR practically throws up.*)

VICTOR. Alka-Seltzer?

(*OSCAR nods his head. VICTOR prepares the seltzer, then
opens the manuscript at the appropriate page.*)

VICTOR. I'm ready.
OSCAR. Wait. Give me a few minutes. (*HE points to
the seltzer.*)
VICTOR. It's ready. (*HE hands it over and OSCAR
drinks.*)
OSCAR. More coffee.
VICTOR. (*Refills his coffee cup.*) You ready?
OSCAR. You can start. By the time Albert's on his
feet, I shall be on mine.
VICTOR. (*Reading.*) "It was raining, and dark clouds
hung heavy in the sky. Though it was mid-morning, there
was little light outside, as though the day had had enough
of itself."
OSCAR. Just how I feel.
VICTOR. (*Reading.*) "It was depressing to view. So
slowly Albert rose ..."
OSCAR. So soon? (*HE staggers to his feet and walks
to his desk.*)
VICTOR. (*Reading.*) "... and paced the room. He
reckoned his years. One hundred and two. He had been
alone for almost half a century. Five wives ago. Five
alimonies past."

OSCAR. Jesus!

VICTOR. (*Reading.*) "He wondered what was wrong with women. He dared not think for one moment that something was wrong with *him*."

OSCAR. Quite right too.

VICTOR. (*Reading.*) "He recalled the end of the last of his marriages. Sandra. She too, like the others, had left him. Not one of the five had died on him. Nothing as respectable as that. In all their health and strength, they had had enough of him. He recalled now those desperate months when he was alone for the first time."

OSCAR. If Albert's going to wallow in self-pity, I'm not going to listen.

VICTOR. (*Ignoring and reading.*) "When a man is in despair he resorts to two things. The cliché and the astrologer. And often both. Every cloud has a silver lining, Albert intoned each morning on waking. And after winter comes the spring accompanied his dressing. But when he heard himself say, My despair is part of life's rich tapestry, he knew he had reached rock bottom. He combed what was left of his hair and went to see a clairvoyant."

(VICTOR rummages in one of the cartons and brings out a grey bald wig which HE hands to Oscar.
OSCAR obediently puts it on.
For himself, VICTOR takes a silk turban and puts it on his head.)

VICTOR. (*To Oscar.*) Come on.

(LIGHTS dim on office and LIGHT the inset stage. In it is a table on which is a crystal ball. Two chairs. Enter VICTOR in turban and settles down.)

VICTOR. *(Calling.)* Next please.

(Enter OSCAR in wig, carrying his coffee cup which HE puts on the table.)

VICTOR. *(Indian accent.)* Not please on the table. It disturbs the aura.

(OSCAR puts the cup on the floor.)

VICTOR. Now place your hands around the ball. Relax. Empty your mind. Loosen the fingers. Do not grip the bowl. Caress it … yes, yes. I feel the vibration. Oh what a sad man you are. But every cloud …
VICTOR and OSCAR. *(Together.)* Has a silver lining.
VICTOR. Ah, I see the dark cloud passing. Very soon. Oh it is beautiful.
ALBERT. What? What?
VICTOR. There is a great adventure soon. Very pleasurable. It clears. I see it clearly now. There is a …

(TELEPHONE rings.)

VICTOR. *(Springs up.)* That's Brenda.

(HE throws off his turban and rushes off the inset stage to the phone on Oscar's desk. OSCAR turns round and boggles at the confusion.)

ALBERT. (*Angry.*) What could you see. What was the adventure?

VICTOR. (*On phone.*) Yes, yes, I'll pay for the call.

(ALBERT comes out of inset stage.)

OSCAR. (*Watching him.*) You've got a nerve.

VICTOR. (*On phone.*) Brenda? Is that you Brenda? (*Pause.*) I just want to make sure I'm not speaking to your rotten mum.

(Pause.
Throughout the conversation OSCAR reacts accordingly.)

VICTOR. (*Angry.*) Why didn't you talk to me yesterday? If I ring you up I expect you to come to the phone? (*Pause.*) What do *I* want? You're ringing me. (*Pause.*) I just ... I want you ... (*Shouting.*) Well I damn well think you ought to come home. (*Pause.*) What d'you mean, why? You're my wife, that's why. And they're my children. (*Long pause.*) You'd better come home or else. (*Pause.*) You'll see. (*Pause.*) What's the weather like out there?

(OSCAR fairly hemorrhages.)

VICTOR. It's nice here too. Yes. (*Pause.*) They can swim. (*Pause. Shouting.*) They have to wear water-wings, d'you hear?

OSCAR. This is enough. This is enough. This is enough.

VICTOR. (*Gently.*) Come home Brenda. (*Pause, shouting.*) I don't want any of your bloody conditions. You come home, d'you hear me? (*Pause, then to Oscar.*) She put the phone down.

OSCAR. I don't wonder.

VICTOR. It's 104 in the shade in Sydney.

OSCAR. That's just abut the same as my temperature. (*Pause.*) You don't know how to handle women. (*Pause.*) Look, let's get on with it. Get back to work. It'll take your mind off Brenda. Your Albert keeps saying, whenever he gets in trouble, and God knows that's often enough, he says work is the only salvation. (*To himself.*) Even dentistry.

VICTOR. I should have stopped her going in the first place. If only I'd ...

OSCAR. If only I'd done this, if only I'd done that. All of us can say that. Any time. In hindsight every man has 20-20 vision. So forget the "shoulds" and the "if onlys" and let's get back to work. I want to know about the adventure. Here, put your turban back on. (*HE hands him his turban.*)

(*VICTOR goes reluctantly to inset stage. OSCAR follows and THEY take their places as before.*)

VICTOR. Where was I?

ALBERT. An adventure for me ... I mean for Albert. You could see a great adventure.

VICTOR. (*Back to Indian accent.*) I need time to re-orientate. To feel the aura.

(HE places his hands on the globe, then takes them away. ALBERT waits expectantly.)

VICTOR. It's gone. The glass is empty.

ALBERT. *(Irritated.)* Are you sure? Look again. Look carefully. *(A moment of perception.)* Jesus, what am I saying? What am I getting so excited about?

VICTOR. It comes. It returns. An adventure. I see an office. I see a man with a strange machine. *(Pause.)* That's all.

ALBERT. *(Disappointed.)* That's the adventure? What kind of machine?

VICTOR. It looks like a computer.

ALBERT. *(Pissed off.)* A computer. Some adventure. Maybe I'm going to the moon.

VICTOR. What're you getting so ratty about? If it's not in the ball, it's not in the ball, and I can't put it there. Anyway, it'll be in the next chapter, I'm sure. Look, let's set it up. Just in case. This is an office. *(HE reaches down and picks up a small computer and puts it on the table.)* Let's leave it here so it's ready.

ALBERT. *(Nonplussed.)* Ready for what?

VICTOR. You've got to set things up. Then things happen. That's how you write a novel. Let's go. Keep your wig. You'll need it later.

OSCAR. *(Helpless.)* I think I'm going mad. I need a drink. What's the time?

VICTOR. Eleven o'clock.

OSCAR. It's too early. *(Pause.)* I'll have one anyway.

(VICTOR pours him a drink and hands it to him. HE guides him to his desk, then goes to his own and picks up the manuscript.)

VICTOR. (*Reading.*) "Poor Albert. He had set so much store by the clairvoyant, who in concrete terms, had offered him nothing. Yet he had given him the *promise* of pleasure, and that lightened his spirits a little. He knew that the core of his misery was loneliness, and that somehow or other, he must seek out company. And to that end, he took himself to one of the numerous matrimonial agencies, the address of which he found in a high class magazine, with the assurance that they would find for him a better class of person. Moreover, it was a French concern with headquarters in Paris. He took much time with his toilette. He was intent on making a good impression. When he looked in the mirror, it was only his body he viewed. That part of him, expensively clothed, belied his age.

(OSCAR mimes this action.)

VICTOR. He avoided any glance at his face, for in no way could he disguise the lines that the years had notched around the eyes, mouth and brow. Not to mention his hairline, which was not visible enough to be mentionable. Yet even without the aid of a mirror, he knew that his beard needed trimming, and this he set about to do with a small nail-scissors.

(While OSCAR is doing exactly that, VICTOR exits and re-appears on the inset stage as the LIGHTS dim on OSCAR and LIGHT on VICTOR.
VICTOR sits at the computer. HE looks up.)

    VICTOR. *(French accent.)* Entrez.

(Enter ALBERT.)

    VICTOR. Name please.
    ALBERT. Albert Smith.

(VICTOR punches some keys very quietly, and precisely, an action HE takes after each response of OSCAR to his various questions. The dialogue has the timbre of two robots in automatic exchange.)

    VICTOR. Age?
    ALBERT. Sixty.
    VICTOR. Occupation?
    ALBERT. Dentist.
    VICTOR. Income group? Rich. Poor. Middling.
    ALBERT. Middling.
    VICTOR. Your likes? What you like.
    ALBERT. Homemaking, cooking, classical music.
    VICTOR. Your dislikes? What you don't like.
    ALBERT. Noise. Ambition.

(VICTOR gives a final flourish on the machine and a receipt issues from its mouth. VICTOR tears it off and flourishes it.)

VICTOR. (*Reading.*) "Victoria Whitworth." A marriage made in heaven.

(*HE hands the ticket to ALBERT and THEY bow to each other. Then BOTH leave.*
LIGHTS dim on inset stage. LIGHTS on office. VICTOR is reading from the manuscript. OSCAR listens at his desk.)

VICTOR. (*Reading.*) "Thus was Albert fixed up with a marriage partner. But before he pledged his troth, he took upon himself the search for a mistress, for he knew that no marriage was complete without one. Once again, he took himself to the French establishment."

(*VICTOR passes over to OSCAR another wig, a red-haired one this time, and together THEY enter the inset stage. THEY sit down and the scene is enacted as before.*)

VICTOR. Name?
ALBERT. Alistair Fairbanks.
VICTOR. Age?
ALBERT. Fifty.
VICTOR. Occupation?
ALBERT. Film producer.
VICTOR. Income? Rich, poor, or middling.
ALBERT. Rich. Very rich indeed.
VICTOR. Your likes? What you like.
ALBERT. Disco dancing. Eating out.
VICTOR. Your dislikes? What you don't like.
ALBERT. Silence. Lack of ambition.

(VICTOR gives a final flourish to the machine and a receipt appears. HE flourishes it and reads:)

VICTOR. *(Reading.)* "Victoria Whitworth." A marriage made in heaven.

(Inset stage BLACKS out. Over this:)

VICTOR. *(V.O.)* "Poor Albert was deeply puzzled. He was faced with two conclusions. Either the agency had only one lady on their books, or ... but the alternative was unthinkable. Yet he *had* to think about it. He had to acknowledge the possibility that no marriages were made in heaven, and that within certain ill-defined parameters, anybody would do for anybody.

(LIGHTS on publisher's office.
OSCAR and VICTOR at their desks.)

VICTOR. *(Reading.)* "It was a terrible blow to his self-esteem. But anything was better than nothing, and in due course, he married Victoria Whitworth, that poor benighted lady who was going to have to do for what was legal and what was not."
OSCAR. Fool!
VICTOR. *(Reading.)* "And of course it didn't work. Albert was desperate. Life was dull in the extreme. And to make matters worse, Victoria had appalling teeth."
Listen, I've got to go for a pee.
OSCAR. Oh, so you're human after all.
VICTOR. *(Rummaging in the dressing-up box.)* Put this white coat on and get into the book. I won't be long.

(Exit VICTOR.
LIGHTS dim on office and come up on inset stage. On it a
*   dental chair.*
Enter HARRIET (now VICTORIA WHITWORTH).
ALBERT enters carrying white coat.)

ALBERT. Victoria, I didn't expect to see you here. (*HE kisses her.*)

VICTORIA. I needed to come up to town to see the dentist.

ALBERT. It's good to see you, Harriet.

VICTORIA. You're so rarely home nowadays.

ALBERT. Well you know how it is. Conferences, sales. And it was *your* idea to move to the country. It's such a long drive. (*Pause.*) Have you heard from the kids?

VICTORIA. Simon rang from Oxford. He's O.K. In the middle of exams.

ALBERT. And Penny?

VICTORIA. She's still busy finding herself. Takes after you. (*Pause.*) Aren't they in touch with you at all?

ALBERT. (*Sadly.*) No. I hope Penny doesn't marry someone like me.

VICTORIA. I managed. I learned to put up with it. Still learning I suppose. Or am I? Do I have to go on learning?

ALBERT. I need time, Victoria. You know that.

VICTORIA. (*Gently.*) What is it now? Twenty years? Twenty years I've been giving you time? And I still don't get the message. (*Pause.*) Or I daren't get it.

ALBERT. (*His arm around her.*) No, it's not like that. I ask you for time, and God knows I've asked for it, often enough. But it's what you've *got*. It's what none of the others have. Time. And we have it together. We have a past. A shared past. We share an unwillingness to reject the past. That's where you score. Above all the others.

VICTORIA. (*Lovingly.*) I suppose now I shall never leave you. (*Pause.*) Will you come home this weekend?

ALBERT. I've ... I've got to go to Rome ... er ... conference.

VICTORIA. (*Weary.*) I'll be late for my dental appointment.

(SHE sits in the chair.
ALBERT puts on his white coat and stands by her side.
Enter DEBORAH (now WENDY) his assistant in white coat. SHE hands him a series of cotton wools which HE stuffs, none too gently, behind VICTORIA's gums. With one hand, ALBERT deals with VICTORIA, while with the other, HE fondles WENDY's neck and much more.)

ALBERT. There my dear. You have to keep your mouth open for five minutes. Keep still. Don't worry. I'll put the sucker in so's you won't want to swallow. Five minutes, dear.

(A GURGLING sound from the water as ALBERT slinks behind the chair, and practically stripping Wendy, mimes opening the door, HE takes her off the inset stage.
After a beat, VICTORIA begins to wriggle uncomfortably, groans and practically chokes on the sucker. Then she's had enough. SHE takes the sucker out, and one by one,

the mimed pieces of wadding wedged in her mouth.
Rises from the chair, and goes to exit of inset stage.
Mimes opening the door, then gives a loud SCREAM.
LIGHTS *dim on inset stage, and LIGHT on office.*
OSCAR sits at his desk.
VICTOR is reading.)

VICTOR. "Poor Albert. He lost not only Victoria, but Wendy too. And not a little alimony. But worse than all of these, he was struck off the dental register. It was Wendy, bereft of all hope and expectation, who charged him with rape, and in view of Albert's past history, the judge was more than ready to believe her.

OSCAR. Well at least he's stopped being a boring dentist. What now?

VICTOR. That's the next chapter. I think we ought to take a break.

OSCAR. Ah, suspense. Well I reckon I can wait. The need to know what Albert Smith does after dentistry, I find faintly resistible. I mean no offence. It just seems to me his occupation is irrelevant.

VICTOR. Good. It's meant to be. Because whatever a man like Albert Smith does for a living, he would still be a non-committing man.

OSCAR. Here we go again. Even if he were a missionary?

VICTOR. *Especially* if he were a missionary. Such a vocation is a handy and very respectable excuse for not confronting one's *self*.

OSCAR. Well I'd buy that one, I suppose. I'll even drink to it. What's the time?

VICTOR. Eight o'clock.

OSCAR. More to the point, what page are we on?

VICTOR. Two thousand odd. I suggest we snatch a couple of hours sleep. Tomorrow's Tuesday.

OSCAR. I wonder if Deborah went to Paris.

VICTOR. Get some rest. Cocoa? Brandy?

OSCAR. D'you know, you must be the first writer in history who ever looked after his publisher. Brandy, please.

VICTOR. You're not exactly my publisher. (*VICTOR hands brandy to Oscar.*)

OSCAR. And you? Will you join me?

VICTOR. No. I have to get in training for the last lap.

OSCAR. (*Raising his glass.*) Well here's to Albert, who I allow to sit down while I'm sleeping. How old is he now, in his reminiscences?

VICTOR. About sixty.

OSCAR. Forty-two years to go. What can *happen* to a man after sixty? It must be down hill thereon.

VICTOR. Lots of things. Fantasy, longings, "if onlys." (*Pause.*) Impotence.

OSCAR. Can I pass on that one?

VICTOR. We're going to weather it to the end. Both of us. (*HE ruffles Oscar's hair.*) Sleep well.

(*LIGHTS dim.*)

Scene 2

Monday night through.
VICTOR is pouring from the thermos of coffee. HE goes to wake Oscar.

VICTOR. It's midnight, Oscar. We'd better get on with it.

OSCAR. (*Wakes up sleepily and takes the coffee offered.*) Where are we?

VICTOR. In your office.

OSCAR. I mean in the book.

VICTOR. Albert's been struck off the register.

OSCAR. Oh yes. And what will he do now? Read on, Victor. I am prepared for all surprises.

VICTOR. You ready?

OSCAR. Go ahead.

VICTOR. (*Reading.*) "Chapter 54. In old age, the past is always the present. Constantly."

OSCAR. I told you it would be downhill from now on.

VICTOR. (*Reading.*) "In his recollections, Albert had now reached those black years, which he would have preferred to gloss over, or to ignore entirely, as if they had never been. But gloss over to what event? Skip to what future?

OSCAR. I told you so.

VICTOR. (*Reading.*) "Often during his years in the nursing home, some small insignificant thing, a taste, a smell, a glimpse through his window, had beckoned him into the tunnel of those black years, and always he had ignored the call. But now, with Death so patently on its already tardy way ..."

OSCAR. And thank God for that.

VICTOR. "... he knew he could ignore it no longer. He had to acknowledge his life in its entirety, and that included those shameful years. For shameful they were indeed."

OSCAR. (*With interest.*) Oh yes?

VICTOR. (*Reading.*) "Albert Smith was a very lonely man. He had come to loneliness late in life, and had never learnt the grammar to handle it."

OSCAR. Oh a terrible phrase that.

VICTOR. D'you think so? I could re-write it.

OSCAR. Don't bother with it now, for God's sake. Mustn't keep Death waiting.

VICTOR. "... the grammar to handle it."

(*OSCAR winces.*)

VICTOR. (*Reading.*) "His loneliness depressed him in the extreme. So long out of practice of company, he was now faintly wary of his performance, and that was even more depressing. He knew he had to test himself, but he was wary of that too. Especially of failure. So he sought out the company of those he would never have to see again, those unknown shadows, with the night as his cover." (*VICTOR takes a policeman's helmet out of the box.*)

OSCAR. What the hell are you doing with that?

VICTOR. I'm a writer, a keeper of Law and Order.

OSCAR. I've heard of writers being lots of things, but in all my years as a publisher, that's a new one on me. What law and order are you keeping, anyway?

VICTOR. Let's go into the book and see.

(*LIGHTS go up on inset stage.*
VICTOR plods on.
One lit lamp-post stands on either side of the stage. Draped around one of these is HARRIET (now GWYNETH). Around the other is DEBORAH (now IVY).

VICTOR. 'Evening, Ivy.

IVY. 'Ullo, luv.

VICTOR. (*Cocking his head at Gwyneth.*) Not seen her before.

IVY. Me neither. Not from round 'ere.

VICTOR. Shall I turn a blind eye then?

IVY. Be a dear.

VICTOR. For the usual consideration?

IVY. Why not?

(HE walks around the stage, skirting Gwyneth, then off.)

IVY. 'Aven't see you around before.

GWYNETH. (*Welsh accent.*) No. My first time.

IVY. First time *ever*?

GWYNETH. No. Worked in Cardiff. Down the docks. First time in London. You don't mind do you, this beat, I mean?

IVY. No. I'll be packing it in soon. One more tonight then I've made my rent. And that's it. (*Pause.*) Been on the game long?

GWYNETH. Years. Can't remember doing anything else.

IVY. How d'you start?

GWYNETH. Accidentally really. I was going to Swansea to see my friend and I lost my purse on the train. I was stuck without a penny. A man said 'e'd give me ten bob. In those days it was a fortune. I was a bit nervous but then I thought (*Laughing.*) I'd been doing it for nothing with men I didn't like, I might as well get paid for it. After that it was easy. It seemed daft to give it away.

It's a funny business. You sell it, and you've still got it.
Can't be many businesses like that.

(THEY laugh together.)

IVY. Not much around tonight. And the pubs closed
hours ago. There'll just be the oldies now. Ashamed to
come out in the light.

GWYNETH. I had an oldie last week. Down at the
docks. He wanted to chat. Talk, talk. That's all. Said he
thought there should be more cuddling about. Said cuddling
was underrated.

IVY. Another way of saying they can't get it up, poor
buggers. Get quite hairy some of them. Want to make it a
law to cuddle.

GWYNETH. Then there's the ones who want to talk
dirty. Verbals I call them. Rhymes with gerbils. That's
what they look like.

(THEY laugh again.)

IVY. Eh, there's one coming now. A right old cuddler
'e looks. 'E's yours. 'Ave your first one in London on me.
(IVY turns and walks to side of stage and watches.)

*(Enter ALBERT walking slowly with the aid of a stick.
HE walks by Gwyneth a number of times, until at last
SHE solicits him.)*

GWYNETH. *(Overloud.)* How about some fun then.
Grandad?

(ALBERT hesitates, walks by, then returns.)

GWYNETH. *(Without fun.)* How about some fun?

(ALBERT whispers in her ear.)

GWYNETH. Oh there's lovely it is. That'll be fun too. Follow me then. *(SHE looks across at Ivy and mouths:)* Verbal!

(After a beat, enter VICTOR.)

VICTOR. She got fixed up then. No more business tonight, Ivy. I've looked around and it's going to rain anyway. Coming?

IVY. Might as well then. Come on cock.

(THEY go off arm in arm.
LIGHTS dim on inset stage and up on office.
OSCAR crosses stage, taking off his wig and sits at his desk.
VICTOR does likewise.)

OSCAR. Those women. I'm sure I've seen them before.

VICTOR. You have. They're all of womenkind. Wives, mothers, daughters, mistresses, nieces. Even grannies.

OSCAR. Rubbish. You're talking like that because you're furious with your wife. You're writing out all your pain, all your hate, all your despair. It's not fiction. It's therapy. And novels are not made for that. Any more than they are for messages.

VICTOR. (*Riled.*) It's nothing to do with my wife. For all I care she can go to hell.

OSCAR. Look at you. Look at your anger. How can you write in such anger. In hot rage there is no perspective. Cool it. It's too soon to write about Brenda.

VICTOR. You leave Brenda out of this.

OSCAR. A writer must write in last year's blood.

VICTOR. Now you sound like a book-reviewer.

OSCAR. (*Seeing him upset.*) Come on, Victor. Look, I may be wrong, but in any case people like ... er ... Albert don't go to prostitutes.

VICTOR. That's exactly where Albert would go. With a prostitute you don't have to commit. You don't have to ask them to give you time. They *sell* it to you. By the hour.

OSCAR. Well what comes after that? Surely that's rock bottom. And he's got forty odd years to go.

VICTOR. You're being judgmental, Oscar. What's the moral difference between buying and selling, if what you're buying and selling is a service.

OSCAR. I have problems in that area.

VICTOR. You won't when you're Albert's age. You'll be grateful.

OSCAR. God help me.

VICTOR. Shall I go on?

OSCAR. I'm listening.

VICTOR. (*Reading.*) "His health had begun to fail him."

OSCAR. I don't wonder. Gallivanting around at night at his age.

VICTOR. (*Reading.*) "He found difficulty with walking and he was obliged to keep himself indoors."

OSCAR. Oh God, he's going to sit down again.

VICTOR. (*Reading.*) "Yet his manly appetites showed no signs of waning. On rare occasions, when he was confined, through sickness, to his bed, those appetites decreased, yet he clung to them on the basis of the *principle* of craving. He felt he *ought* to feel desire, he *ought* to crave it. The appetite might well shrink, but that principle he would never abandon. So, house-bound now, he was forced to take his pleasures with his own company.

OSCAR. Jesus! We're not going to have a chapter on *that* solitary pursuit.

VICTOR. Only in what *promotes* it. Only the ammunition needed for its success. In other words, the imagination.

OSCAR. (*Wearily.*) Another interior monologue. Another three pages of non-event.

VICTOR. There are a million more plots and happenings in fantasy than there could ever be in fiction. Fantasy is bound by no limit, no grammar, no rules of syntax or tense.

OSCAR. Well weave away, Victor. Thicken the plot and try me.

VICTOR. (*Reading.*) "Alone at the window, Albert conjured up the stirring images of his past. But no single image would hold for long. It would blur into another with no respect for texture or indeed chronology. Calendar has no place in fantasy. He conjured up not images, but a kaleidoscope. He was confused, and he wondered whether or not he was going mad. But at the same time, he knew that it was his last chance for sanity.

(*LIGHTS dim on office.*

*LIGHT up on inset stage. All the symbols of the former
inset cameos are assembled there. The bed, the
computer, the crystal ball, the dental chair, the portrait
of Freud, and the two lamp-posts either side of the
stage.*
*HARRIET enters and stands behind the computer. SHE
wears her Scene 1 dress.*
*After a beat, enter DEBORAH, also in Scene 1 dress, and
stands beside Harriet.)*

HARRIET. (*Angry.*) What are you doing here. You've
no right.

DEBORAH. I'm part of his fantasy. Just like you.
Manipulated. Both of us.

(Pause.)

HARRIET. Why do you do it? You and your kind.
Can't you find someone who isn't married?

DEBORAH. I didn't look for Oscar. He found me.

HARRIET. You could have said no. (*Pause.*) I bet
you're active in the Women's movement.

DEBORAH. As a matter of fact I am.

HARRIET. What's all this talk about sisterhood then?

DEBORAH. That's got nothing to do with anything.

HARRIET. No, only when it's convenient.

DEBORAH. Look, I'm sorry. But even if I go away, it
won't make all that difference. There'll be someone else.
You know it.

HARRIET. (*Bitter.*) Oh yes, I know it. I've been
married to him for years and you must be at least the
thirteenth woman I've given him time for.

DEBORAH. He'll never leave you, you know.

HARRIET. What makes you so sure?

DEBORAH. Because you're a victim. You're innocent, and that makes him more guilty. That's why he stays. Much more interesting is why you haven't left *him*.

HARRIET. I couldn't tell you that either.

DEBORAH. You're a masochist, that's why. You know, one thing I learned in the Women's movement. About masochism. Jesus, what a weapon. Masochism is the search for control, and women are pretty good at it. (*Pause.*) Here he comes, poor sweetheart. I think this chapter's going to be very sad indeed. Poor old Oscar has only got himself to play with. Let's be kind to him.

(*Enter ALBERT. HE takes up his position between the two women behind the computer. This scene is played in a masturbatory rhythm.*)

ALBERT. (*To Harriet.*) One.

(*HARRIET presses a key.*)

ALBERT. (*To Deborah.*) Two.

(*DEBORAH presses a key.*)

ALBERT. (*To Harriet.*) Three.

(*Another key.*)

ALBERT. (*To Deborah.*) Four.

(Likewise. And so on. HARRIET and DEBORAH continue
to recite and type the figures rhythmically throughout
the scene.
ALBERT hobbles over to the portrait of Freud, takes it
down and places it in the dental chair.)

ALBERT. *(To Freud.)* Now you just wait there. Keep
still. Keep your mouth open. Five minutes. I'll be back.
(HE goes to the front edge of inset stage and pokes his head
out. Calling.) Victor, why aren't you in here?
VICTOR. *(Shouting.)* I only manoeuvre fiction. I can't
interfere with fantasy. You're on your own, Albert. Get
weaving.

(ALBERT returns to the dental chair. As HE passes the
computer, HE pauses and listens.)

HARRIET. Fifty.
DEBORAH. Fifty-one.
ALBERT. *(Crosses to the dental chair.)* You can shut
your mouth now. *(HE takes the portrait and leans it*
carefully against the lamp-post. To picture.) There. Now
you can charge by the hour and make an honest living.
(ALBERT crosses over by the bed and again pauses by the
computer.)
HARRIET. Seventy-five.
DEBORAH. Seventy-six.

(ALBERT staggers towards the crystal ball, picks it up,
and hobbles towards the bed. There HE lies down,
cradling the ball in his arms.)

VICTOR. (*V.O., shouting.*) How you doing Albert?

ALBERT. Almost there.

VICTOR. *What* are you doing, Albert?

ALBERT. I'm going to bed with my future. At least I *know* it's unreliable.

HARRIET. (*Shouting.*) Ninety-nine.

DEBORAH. (*As paen of joy.*) One hundred.

(*A long moan from ALBERT. As the LIGHTS dim on inset stage, HE staggers out onto the apron, followed by HARRIET. HARRIET puts her arms around him.*)

HARRIET. Come home, Oscar. You don't need to be given time any more. You can be on your own with me.

ALBERT. (*HE holds her close.*) Oh, Harriet.

(*LIGHTS on office. OSCAR staggers to his desk taking off his wig. HE looks disconsolate.*)

OSCAR. Give me a break will you.

VICTOR. We're near the end.

OSCAR. Yes but *how* near. If that last scene doesn't kill off old Albert, nothing will. What *is* this man? Immortal?

VICTOR. We're on the last chapter. Death approaches.

OSCAR. And none too soon. I'll miss him though, the old bugger. I have to console myself with the thought that he's had a very long life, and certainly a very active one. What page are we on?

VICTOR. Three thousand. The last.

OSCAR. Take it slowly, Victor. Very slowly. I want to relish it.

VICTOR. (*Reading.*) "Death is the final orgasm."

OSCAR. That's terrible, Victor. You simply cannot get away with that one.

VICTOR. I could re-write it.

OSCAR. It's beyond re-writing. Cut it out altogether. It's banal. Let's have a little *majesty* here. All his life Albert never showed any dignity. He must have been saving it up. Let him spend it now, prodigiously, in facing death. Something noble, something that will uplift the spirit.

VICTOR. Well not quite, I'm afraid. Shall I go on?

OSCAR. Let's hear your version then.

VICTOR. (*Reading.*) "His sight was failing, but it served well enough to recognise the shadow of death's approach. For he could smell it. He stretched out his hands in entreaty, and to his lips came that time-honoured phrase that had punctuated the whole of his life. He looked death squarely in the face, and, as if she were his wife or his mistress, he said, 'Give me time, I beg you.' "

OSCAR. (*Laughing.*) Well there's no harm in asking.

VICTOR. (*Reading.*) "And Death, deaf to entreaty, gently embraced him. (*Pause.*) The end."

OSCAR. I suppose now you're going to tell me he died from non-committal. At the age of one hundred and two, Albert Smith died from an inability to make up his mind. What a wonderful disease. (*Pause.*) I'm pulling your leg, Victor.

VICTOR. It's three in the morning. The hijack's over.

OSCAR. Not really. We haven't talked about the pay-off. Listen, I may be stark raving mad, but I'm going to publish it. It's got something. It'll have to be cut of course, and the title changed, and there won't be much of an advance. The printing costs will be astronomical.

VICTOR. I … I don't think you understand, Oscar.

OSCAR. What d'you mean?

VICTOR. I didn't bring the book here for that reason. I didn't hijack you with publication in mind.

OSCAR. (*Flummoxed.*) Well what the hell did you do it for?

VICTOR. I hijacked you for time. That was my only demand. You gave it to me. I just wanted to read my novel to someone in authority. I wanted someone to listen. That's been done. I don't want it published.

OSCAR. Well now I've heard everything. (*Pause.*) What are you going to do now?

VICTOR. Go to Australia. Bring Brenda home. Write another novel.

OSCAR. (*Gently.*) *Your* form of adultery. Listen. Give me notice of the next one. I'll reserve a long weekend for you. Let's have a drink before we turn in.

VICTOR. You pour it. I'll start clearing up.

(*VICTOR stacks the manuscripts in the cartons, and begins packing the hamper. OSCAR pours the drinks.*)

OSCAR. I'm going to miss you, Victor. Not many writers like you, you know.

VICTOR. What d'you mean by that?

OSCAR. Writers who get their readers involved. I'm not likely to forget your novel for a long time to come.

VICTOR. You'll forget the novel. You'll only remember the hijack.

(By now all is cleared away, except for the glasses that THEY hold.)

OSCAR. To you, my friend.

(VICTOR raises his glass.)

OSCAR. I'm turning in. I can catch a few hours before the office opens. God, will I have a story to tell. What happened to your gun, by the way?
VICTOR. I packed it.
OSCAR. *(Lies on the couch.)* Was it loaded?
VICTOR. Only with my determination.
OSCAR. That's a bad line, Victor.
VICTOR. I'm too tired to re-think it.
OSCAR. You coming to bed?
VICTOR. Soon. You go to sleep. I've still some clearing up to do.
OSCAR. Well goodnight then. Tomorrow morning I'll take you out for a big breakfast.

(OSCAR turns over on the couch.
VICTOR waits then tip-toes across the room, making sure that nothing is left behind. HE opens the door and quietly deposits the crates and hamper outside. With a last look around, HE steals away. No proof of his erstwhile presence remains.)

Scene 3

Tuesday.
LIGHTS come up slowly on office. OSCAR stirs on the
couch, sits up, rubs his eyes, looks around.

OSCAR. (*Calling.*) Victor. (*Pause.*) Victor. (*HE*
examines Victor's desk for any trace of him.) Victor, where
the hell are you? (*Panic threatens. HE goes to the door and*
looks outside. The PHONE rings. OSCAR dashes to it
gratefully. Into phone.) Victor? (*Pause. His face falls. The*
PHONE clicks and OSCAR puts it down. To himself.)
Harriet. (*HE puts his head in his hands. To himself.*) Who
in God's name's going to believe me. He hasn't even left a
paper clip.

(The door opens and DEBORAH enters. HE rushes to her
as some life-line.)

OSCAR. (*Clasping her.*) Deborah.

(SHE frees herself from him. SHE is distinctly unfriendly.
SHE walks straight past him into her office.)

OSCAR. Deborah. What's the matter?

(SHE comes out of the office, still in her coat, a pile of
books in her hands.)

DEBORAH. Nothing's the matter. I've come to collect
my things. I'm leaving. Oh by the way, here's your lousy

ticket. You might get a rebate on it. (*SHE throws it on his desk and makes for the door.*)

OSCAR. (*Rushes to stop her.*) Stop. Listen to me. It wasn't my fault. I couldn't get to the airport. I wasn't allowed to get to the airport. I was hijacked.

(*It sounds as improbable to him as it does to her.*)

DEBORAH. Oh yes, and I was kidnapped by an Italian count.

OSCAR. It's true. A writer. He held me at the point of a gun.

DEBORAH. That's the beginning of a pretty interesting novel, Oscar.

OSCAR. Honestly, Deborah.

DEBORAH. What was his name?

OSCAR. Victor.

DEBORAH. Victor what?

OSCAR. (*Realising it for the first time.*) I … I don't know. (*Angry.*) How should I know. A hijacker doesn't announce himself.

DEBORAH. Pity. You'll need to know that to put it on the jacket. What was it called?

OSCAR. I've forgotten. It was terribly long.

DEBORAH. Perhaps you should go and see a doctor.

OSCAR. (*Angry.*) Listen to me. I don't need any doctor. I was hijacked. I've been here in the office the whole weekend.

DEBORAH. (*Shaking him off.*) That's about enough. You've been in Dorset the whole weekend. With your wife. (*Spitting it out.*) Fishing.

OSCAR. It's not true.

DEBORAH. I rang your house. Your Mrs. Smith told me. (*Imitating Mrs. Smith.*) Mr. and Mrs. Anderson have gone to Dorset for the weekend. Oh she was very chatty. Told me all about your fishing tackle. How she's laid it out. Like a bloody corpse.

OSCAR. *Frantic.* She didn't know. She thought I'd gone to Dorset. That's what she thought.

DEBORAH. Who put the thought into her head? Listen, I've had enough. Three years is enough to make a choice. Well I'm making it now. You can find yourself someone else to give you time.

OSCAR. Deborah, you've got to believe me. I was (*Losing confidence.*) hijacked.

DEBORAH. I think you watch too much television.

(SHE leaves and OSCAR gapes after her. HE panics, and, his back to the door, HE frantically rummages in the waste-paper basket.)

OSCAR. You bastard, Victor.

(Enter HARRIET, unseen by OSCAR.)

HARRIET. (*Controlled.*) Where did you sleep last night?

OSCAR. (*Practically jumps out of his skin. Turns and sees Harriet.*) Harriet. Just … just sit down.

HARRIET. (*Measured.*) I don't need to sit down. I want to know where you slept last night. You could not have come back from Paris this morning. The first plane has only just got in. Don't deny it. I've checked.

OSCAR. I haven't been to Paris. Oh for God's sake, Harriet, *sit down*.

HARRIET. Where have you been?

OSCAR. Sit down. *Please*.

(HARRIET sits down at his desk. OSCAR daren't look at her.)

OSCAR. I've been here all the weekend. I was hijacked.

HARRIET. *(Anxious.)* Oscar, are you alright?

OSCAR. Another one.

HARRIET. Another what?

OSCAR. Nothing. Listen. I was hijacked. A writer came in here with a manuscript. Three thousand pages long. He pointed a gun at me and made me listen as he read his novel.

HARRIET. *(Convinced he's mad. SHE humours him.)* Really, dear. The whole weekend? How did you eat?

OSCAR. He brought a hamper.

HARRIET. *What* did you eat?

OSCAR. Oh you know, sandwiches, coffee, a bit to drink. *(Quickly.)* Not much to drink.

HARRIET. *(Looking around.)* Where are the cups and … er … the crumbs?

OSCAR. He cleared it all away. *(To himself.)* The bastard.

HARRIET. What was the novel called?

OSCAR. Oh … I've forgotten. The title was too long.

HARRIET. *(Patient.)* Well what was it about?

OSCAR. It was about non-commitment.

HARRIET. *(Interested.)* Oh yes?

OSCAR. (*Dangerous ground.*) Well, not really. It was about ... er ... a circus ring-master and all his travelling troupe. (*Gathering momentum.*) They travelled all round the world. France, Germany, Italy, Australia. Australia! He's got a wife in Australia.What's her number? Where's her bloody number? (*HE frantically searches another waste-paper basket.*)

HARRIET. (*Nervous.*) Oscar, control yourself. Where *is* this novel. This three thousand pages.

OSCAR. (*Helpless.*) He took it away.

HARRIET. You rejected it?

OSCAR. Of course I rejected it. It was no good at all.

(*HARRIET has spotted the airline ticket that Deborah has thrown on his desk. SHE examines it as OSCAR waffles on.*)

OSCAR. All that rubbish about animals in the circus and training the lions and ...

HARRIET. (*Enraged.*) Some hijack. (*Waving the ticket.*) To Paris. By Miss Deborah Wooland.

(*Well there's not much OSCAR can do about that one.*)

OSCAR. (*Unable to explain.*) I can explain that too.

HARRIET. (*Rising.*) Don't bother. Don't bother to come home either. I shall see to it that the locks on the door are changed. And I shall send all your things onto your club. (*SHE starts to take her leave.*)

OSCAR. Harriet!

HARRIET. (*With utter contempt.*) What is it you want? More time? (*SHE leaves.*)

OSCAR. (*Looks around him, helpless. After a beat.*) I'm innocent. This time I'm innocent. I can prove it, Harriet. Listen. I even went to a shrink. *He'll* confirm it. And I—Jesus, I must have been mad, I went to a fortune-teller. An Indian. I could find his address. Harriet, you've got to believe me. One night I went out on my own and I ... No I didn't. I most certainly did not. (*Pause.*) Oh God, what's happening to me. (*HE makes to sit down at his desk.*)

OSCAR. No, I mustn't sit down. Sitting only leads to trouble. It leads to nostalgia. And God, that's trouble.

(*Noise of FOOTSTEPS on stairs.*)

OSCAR. (*With delight.*) Harriet?

(*Noise of repeated intoned MANTRA.*)

OSCAR. (*Shattered.*) Oh God, that's all I need.

(*Enter KRISHNA carrying a bucket and brush.*)

OSCAR. You're in late today, Krishna.

KRISHNA. Missed the bus, Mr. Anderson. Will I be in your way?

OSCAR. No. Carry on. I'm going anyway. Just called in for the post. (*HE collects some papers from his desk.*) Have a nice weekend?

KRISHNA. Pretty good. And you?

OSCAR. Yes. (*Pause.*) You know Krishna, an extraordinary thing ... oh, it doesn't matter.

(KRISHNA shrugs. OSCAR makes to leave.)

OSCAR. Be sure you lock up.
KRISHNA. Yes, Mr. Anderson.

(OSCAR leaves.
KRISHNA sprays the desk with polish and starts rubbing.
As he does so, HE scratches his mane. Then slips his
fingers under the wig to scratch his scalp. Nonchalantly
HE takes the whole wig off to scratch, and reveal
Victor's shock of black hair. HE continues to polish as
the LIGHTS dim.)

END OF PLAY

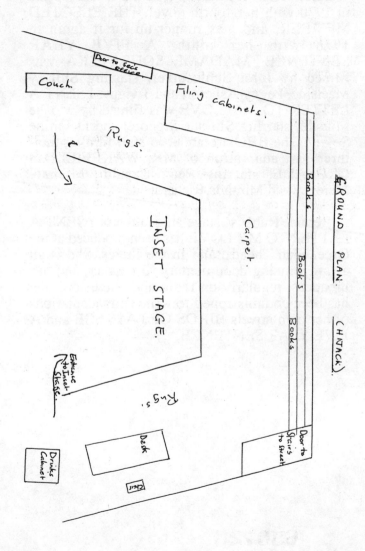

GROUND PLAN (CHTACK).

Door to Secs OFFICE

Couch.

Filing cabinets.

Rugs.

Books

Books

Books

Books

Carpet

INSET STAGE.

Entrance to Inset Stage.

Rugs.

Desk

Drinks Cabinet

Chair

Door to Stairs to Street

Stairs to Street

BERNICE RUBENS won the Booker prize in 1970 with her fourth novel, THE ELECTED MEMBER, and was runner-up for it again in 1978 with her ninth, A FIVE YEAR SENTENCE. MADAME SOUSATZKA was filmed by John Schlesinger, starring Shirley Maclaine, Peggy Ashcroft and Twiggy. I SENT A LETTER TO MY LOVE was filmed by Moshe Misrahi, starring Simone Signoret and Delphine Seyrig. The BBC are about to start filming their three-part adaptation of MR. WAKEFIELD'S CRUSADE, starring Peter Capaldi, Michael Maloney and Miranda Richardson.

Bernice Rubens' stage adaptation of I SENT A LETTER TO MY LOVE has been produced at the Greenwich Theatre and in the States. She is an award winning documentary filmmaker, and has broadcast regularly on radio and television. She has been commissioned to write film adaptations of her own novels BIRDS OF PASSAGE and A FIVE YEAR SENTENCE.